Start to Finish
Second Series

FROM Cub TO Panda

JENNIFER BOOTHROYD

LERNER PUBLICATIONS Minneapolis

Lerner Publications Company
A division of Lerner Publishing Group, Inc.
241 First Avenue North
Minneapolis, MN 55401 USA

For reading levels and more information, look up this title at www.lernerbooks.com.

Library of Congress Cataloging-in-Publication Data

The Cataloging-in-Publication Data for *From Cub to Panda* is on file at the Library of Congress.
ISBN 978-1-5124-1828-6 (lib. bdg.)
ISBN 978-1-5124-1833-0 (pbk.)
ISBN 978-1-5124-1834-7 (EB pdf)

Manufactured in the United States of America
1-41172-23180-3/22/2016

TABLE OF Contents

Pandas are fascinating! How do they grow?

First, the panda gets her den ready.

A mother panda must find a safe place to have her cub. The mother finds a spot at the base of a hollow tree or in a rocky cave. She pulls in branches and plants to make a cozy den.

Next, the baby panda is born.

A newborn panda is very tiny and has pink skin. It can't see, hear, or move. It spends most of its time drinking its mother's milk and sleeping. For the first few days, the mother never leaves the den.

The cub grows black-and-white fur.

When it's born, a panda cub has thin hair. Light gray fur soon covers the skin. Then black hairs grow on the cub's face and legs. In a few months, the cub has all its black-and-white markings.

Soon the cub opens its eyes.

The cub **relies** on its mother for food, shelter, and protection. A newborn panda's eyes stay closed until it is almost two months old. The cub then sees for the first time.

Then the cub explores its habitat.

A newborn panda's legs are very weak. But as the cub grows, it starts to take steps and learns how to crawl without falling over. Sometimes cubs roll on the ground when they play.

The cub starts to eat bamboo.

Around eight months old, the cub still drinks milk, but it is ready to try solid food. Pandas in the wild eat mostly bamboo.

The panda is ready to survive on its own.

Before it is two years old, the cub can survive without its mother. It doesn't need milk anymore and can find bamboo to eat. It knows how to climb a tree if it feels threatened.

Then the panda finds a good place to live.

Pandas in the wild don't spend a lot of time with other pandas. They wander around to find their own place with food and water. They mark the area with their scent to let other pandas know not to stay there.

Finally, the panda can have its own cub.

Pandas are usually old enough to have cubs when they are five years old. But panda cubs are not born often. People work to protect panda cubs to make sure pandas live for many years to come!

Glossary

bamboo: a woody, tall plant

cub: a young panda

den: an animal's shelter

habitat: the natural area where an animal lives

relies: depends on

survive: to continue to live or exist

threatened: at risk of being in danger

Further Information

Boothroyd, Jennifer. *From Cub to Tiger.* Minneapolis: Lerner Publications, 2017. If you enjoy reading about animal life cycles, check out this book to learn how a small cub grows into a huge tiger!

Jazynka, Kitson. *Panda Rescue: All about Pandas and How to Save Them.* Washington, DC: National Geographic, 2016. Learn about pandas and discover ways you can help protect these animals.

San Diego Zoo Animals: Giant Panda
http://animals.sandiegozoo.org/animals/giant-panda
See photos and discover interesting facts about pandas.

Shaw, Gina. *Welcome, Bao Bao.* New York: Penguin Young Readers, 2015. Learn about the panda cub that was born at the National Zoo in 2013.

Smithsonian National Zoological Park: Giant Panda Cam
https://nationalzoo.si.edu/animals/webcams/giant-panda.cfm
Watch live footage of two pandas living at the National Zoo in Washington, DC.

Index

Photo Acknowledgments
The images in this book are used with the permission of:
© iStockphoto.com/GlobalP, pp. 1, 3; © Mitsuaki Iwago/
Minden Pictures, pp. 5, 11; © Katherine Feng/Minden
Pictures, pp. 7, 9, 13, 17, 21; © iStockphoto.com/yesfoto,
p. 15; © Michel & Gabrielle Therin-Weise/Alamy, p. 19.

Front cover: © plavevski/Shutterstock.com.

Main body text set in Arta Std Book 20/26.
Typeface provided by International Typeface Corp.

LERNER
SOURCE

Expand learning beyond the printed book. Download free, complementary educational resources for this book from our website, www.lernerresource.com.